The Last Emperor of China
Published by:
FormAsia Books Limited
706 Yu Yuet Lai Building
45 Wyndham Street
Central
Hong Kong

www.formasiabooks.com

Published 2006
ISBN: 988-98269-3-3
Text © FormAsia Books Limited
Written by Anna Hestler
Edited by Peter Moss
Designed by Format Limited
FormAsia Marketing Eliza Lee
FormAsia Archive Sathish Gobinath
Photographic Research Sabine Fähndrich

Source of photographs:
FormAsia Books: 5, 9-10, 13, 21, 42, 84-85
David Cridland Collection – London: 26
Time/Life – New York: 6
Getty Images – New York: 20, 32-33, 46-47, 67
Hulton/Getty – London: 30
Smithsonian Institute – Washington: 22, 25
Ullstein Bilder – Hamburg: 23, 66, 68-69, 82
Corbis – New York: 24, 31, 80-81
S.V. Bilderdienst – Munich: 27
Magnum – London: 28, 40-41, 43
AKG Images – Frankfurt: 29, 88, 94
Xinhua News Agency – Hong Kong: 44
Xinhua News Agency – Nanjing: 87
Palace Museum – Beijing: 45, 58-59, 60-61, 62-63, 64-65, 83
Sydney Gamble Foundation – New York: 48-49
KMT Archive – Taipei: 86, 89, 90-91
China News Services – Taipei: 92-93
Sovfoto – New York: 95

The Last Emperor of China

Prisoner of history

Anna Hestler

FormAsia

In 1644 the Manchus, or
'northern barbarians' as the
Han Chinese called them, crossed
the Great Wall and swept down
on Peking to overthrow the
flailing Ming dynasty. 'The wheel
of the world has turned,' declared
the Manchu – and Heaven's
Mandate passed to China's last
imperial dynasty, the Ch'ing.

During the first half of the Ch'ing dynasty, the Chinese empire was a model of social stability and good government, and its political philosophy drew admiration from European thinkers such as Voltaire and Montesquieu.

Life flourished in all areas, and China enjoyed a golden age: the empire reached its greatest extent since the days of the Mongol emperors; architecture and the arts thrived; the population multiplied rapidly; and the economy prospered.

By the middle of the eighteenth century, China was not only self-sufficient, but the wealthiest and most powerful empire in Asia. There was nothing that it needed from the outside world, which it treated with condescension.

The success of the Ch'ing dynasty, however, was also the source of its downfall. In time, greed and corruption weighed so heavily on the ruling house that the Celestial Empire began to collapse. Political intrigue and power struggles divided the court and undermined the emperor's authority – and the wheel of the world turned once again.

On 17 October 1967 a bespectacled old man lay on his deathbed in Peking's Capital Hospital. He was aware of the Cultural Revolution that raged outside. A few days earlier a gang of teenage Red Guards had come for him. Miraculously the hospital staff had sent them away on the orders of Premier Chou En-lai. The angry youths threatened to return.

Once again the old man was caught in the toils of history; he could not escape even through death. For when he died none of his relatives dared venture out into the chaos to collect the ashes of his cremated body. His soul remained trapped between Heaven and Earth for twelve years until his family was finally able to hold a formal burial

ceremony for him. His name was P'u Yi.
He had once been the emperor of China.

The life of P'u Yi, the last emperor of
China, is both a tragic tale and a fascinating
chronicle of a nation in transition. Heir to
the 267-year-old Ch'ing Dynasty, P'u Yi
was enthroned as emperor just as his
country was beginning its painful
metamorphosis from absolute monarchy to
party dictatorship. He witnessed it all: from
revolution to chaos, from war to the People's
Republic of China. During these troubled
years, he was caught in the maelstrom
that engulfed China and controlled by the
powers that ruled his country. He led a
privileged but powerless life, virtually
imprisoned by historical events.

Born in Peking on 7 February 1906 P'u Yi was, by birth, a
Manchu of the royal Aisin-Giorio clan. He was the eldest son
of Prince Ch'un II, brother of the nominally reigning Emperor
Kuang Hsu. His mother, Princess Ch'un, was the daughter of a
prominent Manchu general who had been one of the Empress
Dowager's most trusted henchman. P'u Yi's ancestors were
originally semi-nomadic warlords who ruled the remote region
of Manchuria in north-eastern China. In 1644, the Manchu
warriors had swept down from their homeland to overthrow
the Ming dynasty, thus inaugurating China's eighth, and last,
imperial dynasty, the Ch'ing or 'Great Pure'.

The Manchus never made up more than two per cent of
China's population and their rule depended on retaining the
imperial system of government that had been established from
the earliest days of China's dynastic history. This system rested
on a Confucian moral orthodoxy stressing the virtues of
obedience to authority and adherence to ritual and propriety.
At its core was the belief in the Mandate of Heaven,
the heaven-sent right to rule which deemed the emperor Son
of Heaven and entrusted him with the responsibility for 'all
under Heaven'. On condition the emperor behaved wisely and
virtuously, he was worthy of the mandate to govern; however,

should misrule or misfortune befall the empire, he would lose Heaven's Mandate and be overthrown.

By the time P'u Yi was born, the Ch'ing's mandate was on the wane. The dynasty was dominated by P'u Yi's great-aunt, the Empress Dowager Tz'u Hsi, who had banished her nephew, the emperor Kuang Hsu, to a small island on an artificial lake within the Forbidden City for leading a reform movement to modernize education and check corruption. A woman with a taste for power and a talent for retaining it, the Empress Dowager ruled behind various emperors from 1860 by manipulating the rules of imperial succession. Pampered by eunuchs and cocooned in the Forbidden City, Tz'u Hsi represented everything that was wrong with China's ruling hierarchy. She sat idle while famine gripped the countryside, squandered funds set aside for modernizing the navy by building a marble boat on Lake Kunming for tea parties, and blocked political and economic reforms that would have enabled China to keep pace with the rest of the world. By the end of the nineteenth century, China was ravaged by civil strife and much of its trade had fallen into foreign hands. In an attempt to swell the number of her supporters and rid the empire of the 'foreign devils' (the Chinese term for foreigners), Tz'u Hsi foolishly backed the Boxer Rebellion.

The Boxer Rebellion began in 1898 as a peasant revolt against foreigners and the forces of change. All too aware that their animosity could easily turn anti-Manchu, Tz'u Hsi skilfully roused the Boxers into a frenzy under the slogan 'Support the Ch'ing, destroy the foreigner'. In June 1900, the Boxers stormed Peking and besieged the foreign Legation Quarter for fifty-five days until an international relief force arrived and occupied the city. As soon as the first troops entered the city, Tz'u Hsi tossed aside her elaborate finery and fled the palace disguised as a peasant woman, her long talons clipped back and her hair dressed like that of a commoner. Her distraught nephew, the emperor Kuang Hsu, rode behind in a separate cart. Prior to their departure, the old matriarch had lost her temper and ordered that his beloved companion, the Pearl Concubine, be thrown down a well for begging to be allowed to accompany him.

While the Empress Dowager was fretting in the distant Shansi Province over what would become of her precious treasures, Peking was being ransacked by foreign soldiers and officials. Every day, looting parties roamed the streets, helping themselves to whatever caught their fancy. The temptation to plunder was great, since more than half the local population had either fled or been murdered, leaving many homes deserted. After turning the city inside out, Western powers agreed to allow the Ch'ing dynasty to remain on the throne for the sake of stability. But it came at a price. Tz'u Hsi was forced to accept a peace treaty which gave foreigners even more control over China's economy and crippled Peking with an indemnity of $335 million. It was the beginning of the end of the Ch'ing dynasty.

After the Boxer fiasco, Tz'u Hsi reluctantly announced that an overdue programme of reform would begin, and tried to re-establish relations with foreign governments. But it was too little, too late. On 15 November 1908, she suffered a seizure brought on by a picnic lunch of clotted cream and crab apples. After bidding her crumbling empire farewell, the 'Old Buddha' ascended upon the dragon and joined her ancestors. By a strange and sinister coincidence she died exactly one day after Emperor Kuang Hsu, who many believed had been murdered. In the hours prior to the emperor's death, Tz'u Hsi had named her two-year-old grandnephew P'u Yi as tenth emperor of the Ch'ing dynasty and his father, Prince Ch'un, as regent. She could not have imagined that the boy-emperor would be stripped of all power before he was six.

Prince Ch'un II, father of Emperor P'u Yi. Prince Ch'un was appointed as regent on behalf of his two-year-old son in 1908. Disinterested in power and politics, he resigned after the Chinese Revolution of 1911 and pursued his interest in astronomy. He died in 1951.

On the death of his brother, the emperor Hsien Feng,
Prince Kung supported Tz'u Hsi's rise to power in the
Manchu court and acted as her advisor until 1880, when he
was overshadowed by P'u Yi's grandfather, Prince Ch'un I.
Reform-minded and friendly with foreigners, Kung set up
the Ch'ing dynasty's first Ministry of Foreign Affairs.

During her rule, the Empress Dowager Tz'u Hsi squandered the
nation's treasury on fripperies – jewels, banquets, palaces and other
royal extravagances. Her fiscal irresponsibility combined with
retrograde policies sparked widespread opposition to the Ch'ing
dynasty and ultimately hastened its collapse. She is pictured here in
front of the Throne Room in the Forbidden City with her retinue of
ladies-in-waiting and the Grand Eunuch Li Lian-ying, c. 1903

In imperial times, no building could be built higher than the walls of
the Forbidden City, the imperial residence of 24 successive emperors.
Here, the Forbidden City towers above its surroundings – a magnificent
symbol of the emperor's central role as mediator between Heaven
and Earth.

A pair of bronze lions guard the entrance to the Hall of Supreme
Harmony, where P'u Yi was enthroned as emperor of China in 1908.
The male lion's right paw rests on a ball, representing the unity between
Heaven and Earth. The lioness in the suckles her cub through her left
claw which symbolizes protection of the empire.

The Empress Dowager Tz'u Hsi was one of history's most formidable
women – a ruthless Manchu concubine who clawed her way to
the throne in 1861, ruling China for half a century with a mix of
manipulation, intrigue and murder. Here, robed in a gold-embroidered
gown and wearing three-inch-long gold fingernail protectors, she looks
every bit the part of a 'dragon lady', c. 1905.

On 21 August 1860, at the end of the second Opium War,
British and French troops stormed the Taku Forts in northern China.
Thereafter, they occupied Peking and forced the Chinese to agree to
the Treaty of Tianjin, which opened further treaty ports to trade and
allowed European merchants and missionaries to travel inland.

In June 1900, the xenophobic Boxers stormed Peking and
surrounded the foreign legations for fifty-five days.
Here, besieged German troops put up a defense as they
await the arrival of the international relief force.

The Dragon Throne in the Forbidden City's Hall of Supreme
Harmony was the centre from which China's emperors,
the Sons of Heavens, issued commands to their subjects.

Here, in the wake of the Boxer Rebellion (1900),
foreigners irreverently take turns posing on the emperor's
Dragon Throne, tarnishing the seat of imperial power.

After suppressing the Boxer Rebellion, allied trooped made
their way to the Forbidden City – determined to penetrate
the heart of the Celestial Empire. Here, foreign troops
approach the Meridian Gate, the City's main entrance.
The Empress Dowager and her entourage had already fled
through another gate disguised as peasants.

Thousands of mourners throng the streets of Peking
to pay their respects to the Empress Dowager Tz'u Hsi,
who passed away in 1908. Under the large canopy,
the grand matriarch's body was wrapped nine times
by a single strand of pearls and robed in a silk gown
embroidered with gold thread.

Dressed in white, the Chinese colour of mourning,
loyal subjects of the empire kowtow before the coffin of
the Empress Dowager Tz'u Hsi at her funeral in 1908.

The Great 'Within'

On a frosty November night, a procession of palace dignitaries astride Mongolian ponies began wending its way from Prince Ch'un's home, the Northern Mansion, to the Forbidden City. At its centre was a golden mahogany palanquin bearing Peking's new Son of Heaven, P'u Yi. As the palanquin passed through the Meridian Gate and across the Golden Water Bridge, P'u Yi entered a new world. The Forbidden City was a dream-like maze of golden-roofed palaces, majestic halls supported by vermillion pillars, elegant pavilions and shaded courtyards – all laid out with symbolic symmetry, reflecting the emperor's central position in the cosmic order. The dragon motif and the colour yellow were everywhere, symbolizing the emperor's power and virility. Sealed off from the outside world by 10-metre-high ochre walls and untouched by the passage of time, this was the secret heart of the empire, the 'Great Within'. To P'u Yi, it would become a lonely and stifling place.

At dawn on 2 December 1908, P'u Yi was dressed in a yellow silk dragon robe and carried to the Hall of Supreme Harmony to be enthroned as 'Great Emperor of the Great Ch'ing Dynasty'. Perched on his cushioned Dragon Throne, a bewildered little

P'u Yi watched as hundreds of officials attired in ceremonial robes embroidered with white cranes and yellow pheasants took their assigned places. A gong was struck and those present sank to their knees in unison, kowtowing nine times. Throughout the lengthy ceremony, the little emperor struggled to break free and cried: "I don't like it here. I want to go home." As officials went on kowtowing, pledging their lives and their loyalty to the new Lord of Ten Thousand Years, P'u Yi cried louder. Aged courtiers looked on in despair: his cries were not a good omen.

After the coronation ceremony, P'u Yi's life was transformed. He had little contact with his family and rarely saw his father, who was overwhelmed by his new duties. His only companions were eunuchs: beardless men who spoke in high falsetto voices and took short mincing steps when they walked. These were men who had willingly been castrated for the privilege of serving the Son of Heaven and the royal ladies. Much of the life of the Forbidden City depended on the imperial eunuchs, who carried out the majority of its business. They handled official documents, administered the treasury, maintained the palace guard, arranged for audiences with the emperor and performed household tasks. As guardians of imperial customs and traditions, they also protected the heavenly aura that surrounded the emperor by enforcing imperial protocol. Indeed it was possible for eunuchs of the highest rank to exploit their intimacy with the emperor to obtain favours and financial rewards. And many did.

From the moment P'u Yi woke up to the moment he went to bed, everything was done for him by a coterie of crimson-uniformed Eunuchs of the Imperial Presence. They bathed him, dressed him, combed his Manchu-style queue (a long pigtail and symbol of Manchu identity), served his meals, played with him, carried him about in his palanquin and instructed him on palace etiquette. The toddler king's upbringing was supervised by five High Consorts, the widows of the two preceding emperors. Every morning a solemn little P'u Yi would pay the old dowagers a visit in their Eastern Palaces: he would address them as 'mothers', and they would ask if he was well. Then they would tell him to 'Go away and play now, emperor'. When P'u Yi was five, the High Consorts chose a Chinese tutor for him and an astrologer selected an auspicious date to begin his studies, 10 September 1911. It was exactly one month before the Chinese Revolution broke out.

After the Boxer Rebellion (1898–1900), progressive-minded Chinese rose up against the incompetence of their Manchu rulers. Frustrated by the sluggish pace of reform under Prince Ch'un, students, intellectuals and military men formed an anti-dynastic movement spearheaded by Dr Sun Yat-sen, a physician-turned-revolutionary who advocated nationalism, democracy and 'people's livelihood'. As political activism gained momentum, a revolution became inevitable. It began in the south of China on 10 October 1911. One province after another proclaimed independence from the dynasty, and two thousand years of imperial rule came to an end. Three months later, Sun Yat-sen was elected provisional president of the Republican government, Prince Ch'un resigned and P'u Yi lost Heaven's Mandate.

Political Chaos and Confusion

Under the terms of the abdication agreement (the Articles of Favourable Treatment), P'u Yi was permitted to retain his title and live in the Forbidden City with an annual stipend of $4 million; in return, he surrendered the right to rule. The terms were generous because, although the various factions involved in the revolution agreed on the need to modernize China and regenerate the country's political system, they were divided on how to achieve these objectives. Some advocated the creation of a constitutional monarchy, while others campaigned for a clean break with the past. Because the abdication agreement was so favourable, five-year-old P'u Yi did not feel the waves of revolution that had rocked China. His life went on as it had before, while the forces of history swirled all around him.

Almost immediately the new republican government was in trouble because it lacked unity. In 1913, Sun Yat-sen was forced to relinquish his presidency in favour of Yuan Shih-k'ai (the former leader of the Imperial Army), who promptly dismissed the government and attempted to establish his own dynasty. But his plans were thwarted by his rebellious generals and his sudden death in 1916. With the government in a shambles, a series of ex-generals backed by private armies attempted to occupy Peking. Then, on 1 July 1917, one of Yuan's former generals Chang Hsun – known as the 'pigtailed general' because of his Manchu queue – ousted Yuan's successor and proclaimed the restoration of the Ch'ing dynasty. But the restoration lasted less than two weeks. It ended when a republican plane dropped three bombs on the Forbidden City: one wounded a sedan-chair bearer, another startled a group of eunuchs gambling in an alleyway, and the third landed in a lotus pond. For the second time in his life, P'u Yi was forced to abdicate.

By 1919, political extremists were demanding that the republic abrogate the Articles of Favourable Treatment and expel P'u Yi from the Forbidden City. The Manchu court came to the conclusion that a restoration could only be achieved with the help of a foreign power. After much debate, those nearest the Dragon Throne decided that a foreign tutor should be engaged so that P'u Yi could learn a foreign language and establish contact with Western powers that might help restore him to the throne. And so, on 3 March 1919, Reginald Johnston – a senior official of the British Colonial Office – was appointed as P'u Yi's English language tutor. His admittance to the closed imperial court was a privilege that had not been granted to a 'foreign devil' since Marco Polo had entered the service of the Mongol court in the thirteenth century.

A dusting of snow transforms
the Forbidden City into a Chinese wonderland.

In 1908, P'u Yi was enthroned in The Hall of
Supreme Harmony, the Forbidden City's most
important ceremonial hall. A marble ramp,
intricately carved with dragons, marks the path
along which his palanquin was carried.

Although the remuneration of eunuchs was puny, their proximity
to the royal family and the treasures within the Forbidden City
afforded them countless opportunities to top up their income
through bribery and corruption. Henry Cartier-Bresson's famous
1948 photograph captures two of the last remaining eunuchs
at the Forbidden City – still haggling.

Revered by millions of Chinese as the 'father of the nation',
Sun Yat-sen was the pioneer of the Chinese Revolution (1911)
and the first president of the Republic of China. He died
in 1925 greatly respected by both the Kuomintang and the
Communist Party for his life-long devotion to the cause of
an independent and modern China.

After the Chinese Revolution (1911) northern warlord
Yuan Shih-k'ai ousted the republic's provisional president,
Sun Yat-sen, and assumed the office himself. Then, after
dissolving parliament, he proclaimed himself emperor of
a new dynasty, the Hung-hsien. He died shortly thereafter,
leaving China divided between rival warlords.

Manchu princes resign after the Chinese Revolution
of 1911, bringing the government to a standstill and
an end to 2,000 years of imperial rule.

In a patriotic outburst, Peking University students
petition for the expulsion of foreign imperialists in
the wake of the May 4 Movement.

The Foreigner within the Sacred Walls

Born in Edinburgh, Scotland in 1874, Reginald Johnston had impeccable credentials. He had been educated first at Edinburgh University, and then at Magdalen College, Oxford. In 1898, he joined the British colonial service and was posted to Hong Kong before being transferred to Weiheiwei in the Shangtung province of China. Johnston was not the typical expatriate, preferring Chinese to British company. From the moment he arrived in Hong Kong, he set out to discover all he could about the Chinese people and their customs. During his twenty years in China, he learned to speak Mandarin fluently and developed an interest in Confucianism.

At forty-five, Johnston cut a striking figure: tall, portly, blue-eyed with greying fair hair and a ruddy complexion. To P'u Yi, who had never seen a Westerner except in magazines, he was a scary 'old man'. Years after their first meeting, he recalled that his tutor's piercing blue eyes 'made me feel uneasy... I found him very intimidating and studied English with him like a good boy, not daring to talk about other things when I got bored... as I did with my Chinese tutors.' How did the tall, gangling boy emperor appear to Johnston? In his first memorandum to the Colonial Office he wrote: 'He is a very "human" boy, with vivacity, intelligence, and a keen sense of humour. Moreover he has excellent manners and is entirely free from arrogance. This is remarkable in view of the extremely artificial nature of his surroundings and the pompous make-believe of palace routine.'

From day one, Johnston saw the blinkered, corrupt Manchu court for what it was. Yet the traditional side of him was captivated by this 'new world of space and time... old before the foundation of Rome', a place in which the 'manners and rituals of a vanishing past still formed part of the daily routine'. A true monarchist, Johnston felt that China was 'not ripe' for a republic and should adopt a British-style monarchy. Over the course of his life, he would watch with sadness as the old China that he loved so dearly was swept away by the modernizing impact of the Republicans, Nationalists and Communists.

During his time in the Forbidden City, Johnston was the only foreigner to observe and take part in the age-old rituals of the imperial court. He noted that P'u Yi's visits to the schoolroom 'were made the occasion for a kind of state procession'.
At one-thirty every afternoon, the boy emperor was carried to the Palace of Mind Nurture in 'an enormous palanquin draped in imperial yellow' and accompanied by 'a large retinue of attendants'.

On arrival, two Eunuchs of the Imperial Presence escorted him into the schoolroom, which was furnished with a long table and decorated with traditional Chinese paintings. P'u Yi always sat at the end of the table that faced south (according to imperial protocol) and Johnston assumed the honorary position to his left. If P'u Yi's younger brother P'u Chieh happened to join the lesson (which he occasionally did), he would kowtow before the emperor and then take his seat. Formalities over, the lesson would begin.

Forewarned that P'u Yi's mind had a 'floating' quality, Johnston tried to stimulate the boy emperor by using English newspapers and magazines in their language lessons. To these were added informal chats about history, philosophy, politics and the life of the English royal family. The lessons were not very successful, but pupil and tutor entered into a long-lasting friendship. To P'u Yi, who had never ventured beyond the walls of the Forbidden City since his arrival there in 1908, Johnston was fascinating. 'I thought everything about him was first-rate,' he wrote years later. 'He made me feel that Westerners were the most intelligent and civilized people and that Johnston was the most learned of Westerners.'

P'u Yi was so impressed by Johnston that he began to emulate the manners and dress of the British. He took to calling himself Henry – after Henry VIII – and talked of going to Oxford to study one day. He bought all sorts of Western trinkets to adorn himself: watches and chains, tiepins, cufflinks, and so on. One day he showed up for his lesson wearing a bowler hat, gloves and an ill-fitting blue suit. Johnston cringed at the sight of him and the next day brought Peking's best tailor to measure him for a proper set of English clothes. The extent of Johnston's influence was so great his casual reference to Manchu 'pigtails' prompted P'u Yi to snip his off. Conservative courtiers recoiled in horror at such sacrilege and saw it as the end of any hope for the restoration of the monarchy.

As Johnston's influence on the boy emperor deepened, there were other changes which the eunuchs and courtiers disliked. During the course of their lessons, Johnston noticed that his pupil was squinting to read the blackboard and suspected that he was short-sighted. When he suggested to the imperial household that the boy be examined by a foreign ophthalmologist, the 'Forbidden City all but exploded,' recalled P'u Yi. 'The thought of His Imperial Majesty wearing glasses!' wailed the High Consorts. 'Or that His Majesty should be looked at by a foreign doctor!' Nobody in the imperial court would grant permission. But Johnston stuck to his guns, and even threatened to resign over the matter. In the end, P'u Yi insisted on seeing a foreign doctor. With that, he got his first pair of horn-rimmed spectacles.

'Modern' ideas continued to infiltrate the Forbidden City. Concerned that it was unhealthy for a teenage boy to be carried about, Johnston gave P'u Yi a bicycle. The boy was so thrilled with this new mode of transport that he ordered bicycles for some of his eunuchs. Even the more sprightly eunuchs, however, found these 'foreign contraptions' difficult to control and often careened off course into the flowerbeds as they raced to keep up with their high-spirited emperor. As his Western tastes became more sophisticated, P'u Yi decided that the Forbidden City needed its own fleet of cars. These were taken for the first 'test drive' on 30 September 1921, when he attended his mother's funeral. It was the first time he had left the Great Within since his arrival there thirteen years earlier.

Spellbound by Johnston's tales of the 'Great Without', fifteen-year-old P'u Yi began to feel stifled in his cloistered world. While others came and went freely, he was a prisoner in his own palace. 'I grew to hate the sight of the high palace wall,' he said. As P'u Yi's frustration mounted, he began plotting his escape from the Forbidden City. His plan was to go to England and study at Oxford, just like Johnston. With the help of his

brother P'u Chieh, he gathered a collection of imperial treasures
under his robe and bribed the guards at the Gate of Supreme
Harmony to let him pass when the opportunity arose. But on
the night of his escape, the boy learned that the guards had
betrayed him and all gates, inner and outer, had been sealed.
His escape plan foiled, he was disheartened. As he became more
and more despondent, the High Consorts decided to administer
the tried and tested imperial cure-all – marriage.

The Dragon and the Phoenix

In early 1922, sixteen-year-old P'u Yi was presented with
photographs of four eligible girls and asked to choose a wife.
'Their faces were very small and I could not see if they were
beauties or not... I casually drew a circle on a pretty picture,'
he recalled. The girl he chose was Wen Hsiu (Elegant Ornament),
a plain, chubby thirteen-year-old from an aristocratic Manchu
family. The High Consorts tut-tutted. She would make a fine
secondary consort, they said, but not an empress. P'u Yi obediently
selected another girl. This time he picked seventeen-year-old Wan
Jung (Beautiful Countenance), a delicate beauty with porcelain
skin and high cheekbones. She came from a prominent
Manchurian family and had been educated at an American
missionary school. The High Consorts twittered their approval.

News of P'u Yi's wedding sent a wave of excitement through the Forbidden City: at last an occasion where aged courtiers could relive the glorious past. Ceremonial robes and flags were dusted off and a programme of traditional rituals began. The wedding ceremony itself began on 1 December 1922 at 3 a.m., the hour selected as most auspicious by court astrologers. Under the moonlight, a magnificent procession of lantern and flag bearers, dragon-and-phoenix parasol carriers, republican soldiers, palace guards, musical bands and the ceremonial Phoenix Chair carrying the empress paraded through the streets of Peking. On arrival at the Forbidden City, Wan Jung was escorted to the Hall of Supreme Harmony, where P'u Yi was waiting on the Dragon Throne. Once inside, she kowtowed nine times before the Lord of Ten Thousand Years as the imperial decree legitimizing the marriage was read out.

Recollecting his wedding night many years later, P'u Yi wrote: 'I felt stifled. The bride sat on the edge of the bed, her head downcast. I looked around me and saw everything was red… it all resembled a melted wax candle. I did not know whether to stand or sit.' Completely overwhelmed, the emperor rushed out of the room, leaving the bride alone on her wedding night. In his autobiography he later confided that 'I thought if there had been no revolution I would now be starting to rule with full powers. I must recover my ancestral heritage.' Obviously this desire to regain his throne was in conflict with his longing for personal freedom and it would trouble P'u Yi for the rest of his life.

After the wedding, Johnston stopped tutoring his pupil and became an unofficial advisor at court. One of the things that concerned him was the emperor's dire financial situation. The Imperial Household Department which managed his privy purse was inefficient and corrupt. Finding the Republican government's subsidy of $4 million a year insufficient to cover expenses, senior eunuchs had been selling off priceless artefacts. At Johnston's insistence, P'u Yi ordered a detailed inventory of the imperial storehouse. But on 27 June 1923, the night before the scheduled inventory, a fire mysteriously broke out in the Palace of Established Happiness. The hall went up in smoke along with some 2,500 gold Buddha statues, and thousands of priceless books and scrolls. Determined to put a stop to the graft once and for all, P'u Yi issued an edict expelling all 1,000 eunuchs from the Forbidden City, except for a select group of fifty who were retained to serve the royal family. Barely a year later, the Son of Heaven himself would be forced to leave the heart of the Celestial Empire.

P'u Yi (far right) in the gardens of the Forbidden City with his brothers Pu Qi and Pu Jie, and Reginald Johnston – a British diplomat who served as the boy emperor's English tutor and confidant until his abdication from the throne in 1912.

As a young man P'u Yi dreamt of studying at Oxford – a dream
inspired by his English tutor Reginald Johnston, but never
realised. Here, garbed in a well-cut tweed suit, P'u Yi looks every
inch the erudite Oxford scholar.

Unable to elude the ever-watchful eunuchs, a frustrated P'u Yi stands
on the roof of an imperial palace – trapped in the Forbidden City.
This picture was taken shortly before his attempted escape in 1921.

On 3 December 1922, Manchu princess Wan Jung
married Emperor P'u Yi. She wore a traditional
red silk gown and a spike headdress adorned by
two pearl phoenixes for the occasion.

In 1922, this portrait of the moon-faced Manchu
princess Wen Hsiu in ceremonial dress was one of
four photographs presented to Emperor P'u Yi for
the purpose of selecting a wife. At the tender age of
thirteen, she became the emperor's secondary consort.

After being driven out of the Forbidden City in 1924, the imperial family took sanctuary in the Japanese legation before going into exile in Tientsin. Here, Empress Wan Jung (second from right in front row) and Secondary Consort Wen Hsiu pose with Japanese envoy Yoshikawa Kenkichi's daughter (centre).

Throughout most of his married life, P'u Yi remained
indifferent to his beautiful wife, Wan Jung. On a rare occasion,
he shows a touch of tenderness towards the empress, c. 1925

Like a practiced puppet, P'u Yi played many parts in the
theatre of Chinese history. Here, attired in an upturned
white collar and black tie, he wears a suitably mask-like
face on the day of his inauguration as emperor of the
Japanese puppet state of Manchukuo, 24 March 1934.

With her porcelain skin, ebony hair and soft brown eyes,
Empress Wan Jung was an unforgettable beauty.
After her death in a Communist prison in 1940, she came
back to life in a legend that told of a beautiful princess
who rescued peasants imprisoned by poverty.

Eunuchs gather outside the walls of the Forbidden City after
being expelled for looting the Palace of Established Happiness and
then burning the evidence, c. June 1923.

The Dragon flees Peking

In 1924 China entered a new round of civil war, and it was only a matter of time before the fragile Republican government collapsed. On 5 November, northern warlord Feng Yu-hsiang marched into Peking and drove the House of Ch'ing out of the Forbidden City. P'u Yi and his family were given one hour to pack their belongings. They were then escorted to Prince Ch'un's house, the Northern Mansion, where P'u Yi was forced to sign the 'Revision of the Articles of Favourable Treatment', which reduced him to the status of common citizen. Thereafter he was to remain under guard as a state prisoner until further notice. Although P'u Yi had no definite plans about his future, one thing was clear in his mind from the moment he entered the Northern Mansion: 'Come what may, I was going to leave. I had not left a big Forbidden City for one in miniature,' he said, 'particularly when I was in such danger there.'

While P'u Yi was contemplating his precarious future, China was in the throes of post-revolutionary chaos. In Peking, Feng Yu-hsiang was replaced by another militarist; in the north, warlords bickered amongst themselves to establish their own fiefdoms; in the south, Sun Yat-sen reorganized his Nationalist People's Party, the Kuomintang (KMT), with the Soviet Union's help, thus inaugurating an uneasy alliance with the Chinese Communist Party. In the press of Peking, Shanghai and Canton, there were reports of an anti-monarchist group which was campaigning for the execution of monarchists as 'traitors of the republic.'

Understandably, P'u Yi was frightened. He had taken up the habit of smoking, which was then in vogue in China, and soon chain-smoked to calm his nerves. After a couple of puffs, he would stub out his cigarette and light another. When he wasn't smoking, he paced around the room breaking unlit cigarettes between his fingers. Clearly, he was in no state to make any decisions about his future. At this point, Johnston stepped in. Fearing an assassination attempt, he decided the emperor must escape to the Legation Quarter, the foreign-held quarter of Peking. He told P'u Yi of his plan, and cautioned him to secrecy – not even Prince Ch'un or the empress must know.

On the morning of 29 November 1924 Johnston, P'u Yi and his bodyguard, Big Li, discreetly made their way to the courtyard of the Northern Mansion, where a limousine was waiting. The three got in and Johnston gave the driver directions. As the car pulled out of the gates, two policemen jumped on the running-boards and refused to let go. Johnston ordered the driver to accelerate and the limo sped off with the officers hanging on for dear life. On arrival at the Legation Quarter, Johnston went straight to the Japanese consulate, as he had already approached the British and been advised that Her Majesty's Government was unwilling to interfere in Chinese politics. The Japanese minister agreed to the emperor's request for asylum and swiftly transferred him to the Japanese compound. While P'u Yi and Johnston weighed up their limited options, the empress and consort tried to console the distressed Prince Ch'un. They learned of their husband's whereabouts two days later, when the Japanese embassy sent a car for them.

That Reginald Johnston delivered his fledgling into the arms of the Japanese is perhaps the greatest irony of P'u Yi's tragic saga. Had he known that the Japanese were secretly plotting to conquer China, his actions would surely have taken a different course. At the time, few had any inkling of Japan's imperialist ambitions. Britain viewed Japan as a possible Asian ally and a bulwark against Soviet expansion in Manchuria – P'u Yi's ancestral homeland. But Manchuria was the key to Japan's master plan. With a surplus of food production, vast amounts of industrial raw materials and a railroad infrastructure, it was a valued prize and vital to Japan's plan of expansion. When the time came for Manchuria's annexation from China, P'u Yi would be a useful political instrument.

Trapped in Tsientsin

After twelve weeks of incarceration in the legation quarter, the Japanese decided that P'u Yi must leave the republican capital for his own safety. On 23 February 1925, the last emperor of

China and what remained of his court fled into exile in Tientsin, a small, but cosmopolitan treaty port east of Peking. Here they moved into Chang Garden, a two-storey villa surrounded by a two-metre-high wall. From the Japanese perspective, it was conveniently situated in the heart of the Japanese Concession, opposite their secret service. At the time, P'u Yi viewed his escape as the beginning of freedom. Looking back on it years later he observed, 'Little did I know, I had entered the tiger's mouth.'

No sooner was the exiled emperor settled in his new 'palace', than a string of Ch'ing loyalists and former generals requested audiences with him. Among them were a number of petty warlords who promised to restore the monarchy in return for money. 'I cannot remember how much money I spent or how much jade, pearls, and jewellery I squandered in trying to win the friendship of the warlords,' P'u Yi wrote in his autobiography thirty years later. The fact that a Russian Mafioso figure named Semenov received the most money shows just how desperate P'u Yi's search for allies was. But what choice did he have? He could never be restored as emperor of China under the Japanese. In their eyes there was only one Son of Heaven – Emperor Hirohito. Thus, during his first few years in Tientsin, P'u Yi's relations with the Japanese were cordial at best, but certainly not close.

For nineteen-year-old P'u Yi, who had been confined to the

Forbidden City all his life, Tientsin offered more freedom than he had ever known. In spite of being shadowed by Japanese security men, the deposed emperor carried on in high-style decadence. He and his wife (called Elizabeth by the press) became the talk of the town and hardly a day passed when there wasn't a newspaper report on the social engagements of 'Mr and Mrs Henry P'u Yi'. Newspaper circulation figures shot up as readers snapped up copies for the latest picture of the exiled emperor, who might be shown playing golf in a tweed suit, dancing the quick step in tails or playing polo in riding habit and white helmet. The empress seldom posed for these photos and when she did, the public noted that she looked pale and thin.

The emperor's outdated matrimonial arrangement was a constant source of gossip in small-time Tientsin. It was also an embarrassment for P'u Yi's secondary consort, Wen Hsiu. Tired of playing second fiddle to the empress at public receptions, she plucked up the courage to demand a divorce. P'u Yi was furious. No consort in the dynastic history of China had ever made such an outrageous demand. Yet divorce was straightforward under Chinese law if both partners consented, and P'u Yi eventually did. He would never see Wen Hsiu again. She returned to Peking and worked as a teacher until her death in 1950. In her own way, the empress also detached herself from her husband. She was miserable and blamed him for robbing her of her girlhood. But her sense of duty prevented her from leaving him. Instead she sought refuge in opium.

At first P'u Yi turned a blind eye to Wan Jung's addiction and her visits to the opium dens. But when one day she collapsed in the foyer of the Astor House Hotel, he realised something serious was amiss. The news electrified the cocktail circuit, causing P'u Yi such embarrassment that he decided to confine the empress to her quarters from then on. For a beautiful woman in the prime of life, the loneliness was too much to bear. In her despair, Wan Jung began to rely more and more on opium to combat her bouts of depression. As her habit became an addiction, the empress and her marriage began to fall apart.

In the midst of his marital breakdown, P'u Yi was shocked by an incident that made him more determined than ever to regain his throne. After Sun Yat-sen's sudden and unexpected death in 1925, his ambitious military aide, Chiang Kai-shek, had snatched the reins of the KMT. By 1928 Chiang had purged the KMT of Communists, and established his Nationalist government in Nanjing. In the course of Chiang's Northern Expedition to extend his power base, some of his troops ran amok and dynamited the sacred Ch'ing tombs in Hupei Province. Coffins were flung open and skeletons stripped of their jewels. For P'u Yi, a devout Confucianist who regarded his ancestors with deep reverence and offered joss sticks every night to appease their spirits, it was act of sacrilege. To add to the disgrace, rumours circulated that the pearls from the 'Old Buddha's' phoenix crown had ended up on Madame Chiang Kai-shek's shoe buckles.

Reginald Johnston, who had resumed his colonial service after P'u Yi's flight from Peking, rushed to Tientsin to offer his support. He was taken aback by the state of his former pupil, who was emotionally drained and tired-looking. The emperor had not slept or eaten for days. It seemed to me as though he had been in communion with the spirits of his outraged ancestors and that they had urged him to turn away from the China that had disgraced herself…' he wrote in his memoirs. In this state of anguish, P'u Yi made an oath to avenge this affront to his ancestors and regain his throne. It was a decision which sealed his tragic fate.

After the desecration of the Ch'ing tombs, various officers from Japan's Kwantung Army made deliberate contact with P'u Yi as part of a plan to lure him to Manchuria. One such was Colonel Kenichi Doihara, a rotund man with lizard-like eyes, who assiduously began convincing P'u Yi that the day would come when he must rule first Manchuria, and then the whole of China. That day came on 18 September 1931, when the Japanese army used an allegedly Chinese-inspired explosion on the Japanese-controlled South Manchurian Railway as a pretext to occupy the city of Mukden. Within days of what became known as the Mukden Incident, the army had launched a full-scale invasion of Manchuria.

On 30 September, twelve days after the Mukden Incident, the Japanese Colonel Doihara offered P'u Yi the position of head of the independent state of Manchuria, assuring him of a restoration once 'the political situation was settled'. He urged P'u Yi to make up his mind quickly because Tientsin was unstable and becoming a 'dangerous place'. Soon after, the British garrison commander in Tientsin called to congratulate P'u Yi on the 'opportunities' available, which the former emperor incorrectly interpreted as British support for the restoration of his dynasty. A few days later, an emissary of Chiang Kai-shek showed up proposing to revive the Articles of Favourable Treatment. P'u Yi gave the emissary a non-committal answer. Uppermost in his mind was the desecration of his ancestors' tombs and he distrusted Chiang. Befuddled by all these callers, P'u Yi was at odds with himself and did not know in which direction to turn. If only Johnston were here to advise him. By a strange coincidence he was!

Johnston had arrived in Tientsin on 'a rather unexpected'

mission as he referred to it, which P'u Yi assumed was Foreign Office business. During the two-day visit, the former tutor and pupil discussed the Japanese plan. Johnston supported it and was excited by the prospect of the 'boy emperor' returning to the land of his ancestors. He even promised to include a chapter entitled 'The Dragon Goes Home' in his memoirs. The two parted on a sad note, aware that they would not see each other again, as Johnston was returning to England. As a farewell present, P'u Yi presented his old friend with a Chinese fan on which he had copied a T'ang dynasty poem:

> *I want to follow him across the river,*
> *But that river is deep and has no bridge.*
> *Oh, that we were a pair of herons,*
> *That we could fly home together.*

After Johnston had left, P'u Yi mulled over Doihara's proposal and began to have doubts. He consulted his long-time advisors who cautioned him to stay put until the Japanese had secured their power base. The Japanese stepped up the mental pressure by staging 'anti-P'u Yi' riots, convincing him that he must escape to Manchuria to save his life. On the evening of 10 November 1931, the Lord of Ten Thousand Years was disguised as a Japanese soldier and bundled into the boot of a car. It was not quite the escape he had imagined.

For three months after his flight from Tientsin P'u Yi was held incommunicado in Mukden, confined to the top floor of a shabby, run-down hotel. From the disrespectful way the Japanese treated him, he sensed that something had gone terribly wrong. But he could not have known the extent of the confusion surrounding the invasion of Manchuria. The major world powers expressed their alarm at Japan's aggression; so did the League of Nations. Within China, students and workers called on Chiang Kai-shek to declare war on Japan. The Japanese government itself was split over the Kwantung Army's invasion, and it took some convincing before the militants won the day. On 18 February 1932, Japan proclaimed the independent state of Manchukuo, 'Land of the Manchus', under the notional rule of P'u Yi. Of the major countries, only Japan, Italy, and Germany extended diplomatic recognition. Chiang's government denounced it as a puppet state and branded P'u Yi a traitor. Once again he was trapped by historic forces beyond his control.

Few foreigners were allowed into Manchukuo. The Japanese military kept strict control of the administration and fought a continuing guerrilla war with native resistance groups. To develop their puppet state as a war base, the Japanese greatly expanded industry and railroads.

Full of imperial airs but with no imperial mandate, P'u Yi poses with dignitaries after his investiture as emperor of the new monarchy of Manchukuo, 24 March 1933. Although P'u Yi was outwardly in charge of the administration, the state was controlled by the Kwantung army and used as a base for Japanese aggression in China.

P'u Yi with Japanese officials shortly after being installed as
figurehead ruler of the Japanese puppet state of Manchukuo.
The *Manchester Guardian* described the new nation as 'little more
than a polite fiction invented to obscure the fact that Japan has gone
in for imperialism in a big way', c. 1932.

Flanked by Japanese officials and plainclothes detectives,
P'u Yi and his wife, Wan Jung, pose for a quick photo during a tour
of Manchukuo, the Japanese puppet state created after the invasion
of Manchuria in 1931.

Japanese dignitaries celebrate Emperor Hirohito's birthday
in Manchukuo's capital, Changch'un, c.1932.

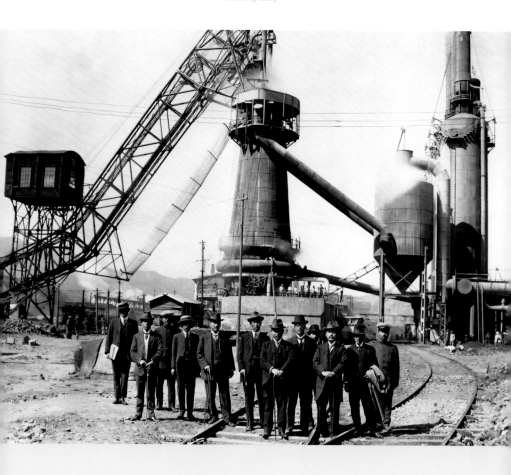

Japanese forces quickly occupy Manchukuo as a base of
their industrial development.

Generalissimo Chiang Kai-shek. During the Chinese Revolution of 1911,
Chiang Kai-shek helped to overthrow the Chi'ng dynasty. Then, in 1928,
he established himself as head of the nationalist Kuomintang (KMT)
government in Nanjing. Although Chiang survived the political storms
of the thirties, his power was constantly undermined by the Japanese on
one side, and the Communists on the other. He fled to Taiwan when
Mao Tse-tung claimed victory for China in 1949.

During the Sino-Japanese War the Japanese overran northern China. In this picture Japanese troops take a break from looting and burning yet another defenseless Chinese city, c. 1937.

In 1937 the Japanese launched a full-scale invasion of China, capturing all the major cities and ports. Japanese troops are shown here entering Nanjing – the seat of Chiang Kai-shek's government. The epic carnage and destruction that followed became known to the world as the Rape of Nanjing.

Japanese troops celebrate by cheering on the walls of the city.
In December 1937 the Japanese occupied Peking, marking the
beginning of the Sino-Japanese War (1937-45).

In 1937, Japan embarked on a full-scale invasion of China
as part of a plan to conquer Asia. Here, Japanese tanks roll
through a village in Hebei Province – there was no-one
to fight because the inhabitants had fled.

A platoon of Japanese soldiers marches towards Nanjing,
the capital of the Nationalist government. After capturing
Manchuria in 1931, the Japanese army advanced south of
the Great Wall, occupying all the major cities and ports.

Mao Tse-tung proclaims the birth of the People's Republic of China
from Tiananmen Square on 1 October 1949. The Communist victory
over the Nationalists, elevated Mao to supreme leader of China and
made his peculiar version of Marxism (Maoism) the official dogma.

With Japan's surrender to the Allies in 1945, P'u Yi was
captured by the Russians and detained in Siberia where
he spent the next five years dreading his return to China,
which had denounced him as a traitor, c. 1945.

In 1960, one year after being repatriated to China,
P'u Yi was given a job in Peking's botanical gardens –
not far from the Forbidden City, but worlds away from
China's imperial past.

From Puppet Emperor to Prisoner

One month after the formation of Manchukuo, P'u Yi was dispatched to its new capital, Changch'un – an industrial city on the north-eastern coast. His new 'palace' was a building which had been the headquarters of the Salt Tax Administration. It was enclosed by a four-metre-high wall. From here P'u Yi reigned over his fictitious state, busying himself with banquets and receptions, ever hopeful that he would regain his throne. But his government had no popular backing, and only a handful of supporters from the racial minorities – the Manchus, Mongols and White Russians. In an attempt to win them over in the face of increasing Chinese resistance, the Japanese decided to enthrone P'u Yi as emperor of Manchukuo in March 1934. 'I went wild with joy,' P'u Yi recalled, and sent for 'my imperial dragon robes'. But the reality of the situation soon crushed his illusions about returning to the glorious past. The Japanese army insisted that, for his coronation, he wear the uniform of the commander-in-chief of the Manchukuo armed forces. It was a portent of ominous events to follow.

In 1935, P'u Yi received an invitation from Emperor Hirohito to visit Japan. He readily accepted and a date was set. On 2 April,

the Japanese sent a 30,000 ton battleship, *Hie Maru*, to escort
P'u Yi to Japan. He wore the dark blue uniform of the supreme
commander of the Manchukuo Navy for the occasion. Four days
later, P'u Yi arrived in Yokohama Harbour to a fanfare of buglers
and a fly past of a hundred Japanese naval aircraft. The welcome
moved him to tears. After disembarking, he travelled by train to
Tokyo where he was personally greeted by Emperor Hirohito.
'I am honoured to be the moon to the Mikado sun,' he said. For
the next eight days, P'u Yi was accorded the respect and attention
he craved. Everywhere he went, he was followed by journalists,
and every day his picture appeared in the papers. There was even
a photograph of him escorting Hirohito's aged mother along the
path in her garden. When it came time for his departure, P'u Yi
told reporters, 'I was deeply moved by the reception given me by
the Japanese imperial family.' He then returned to his fictitious
state to resume his role as puppet emperor.

As the months turned into years, P'u Yi languished in his 'Salt
Tax Palace' while the rest of China lurched towards a new order.
He listlessly rubberstamped Japanese documents, thus giving
his unspoken approval to expropriations of Manchu and
Chinese property and brutalities against innocent civilians.
After 1938, he rarely left his palace and filled his endless days

riding his bicycle round the grounds. Occasionally he saw the empress for meals, but as she passed through the stages of opium addiction she withdrew from reality and the two barely communicated with each other. During this period, P'u Yi became a devout Buddhist, reciting sutras and praying before an image of the Buddha. He also returned to the old ways of the Forbidden City, consulting oracles in the hopes he would receive a 'good omen' – but he never did.

In 1937 P'u Chieh, who had been dispatched to a military school in Japan six years earlier, arrived in Changch'un with his Japanese wife Hiro Saga, second cousin to the Emperor Hirohito. Shortly after, the State Council of Manchukuo passed a succession bill making P'u Chieh successor to the throne in the event that the emperor died childless. P'u Yi saw it as a plot against him and acquired a new consort, Jade Years. She died childless and was replaced by Jade Lute, the twelve-year-old daughter of a waiter from a local restaurant. Convinced that the Japanese had poisoned Jade Years, P'u Yi became paranoid. As the walls of the Salt Tax Palace closed in on him, the Japanese army occupying Manchuria pushed south of the Great Wall.

On 8 July 1937 a full-scale war erupted when Japanese and

Chinese troops clashed on the Marco Polo Bridge near Peking. A few weeks later, on 28 July, the Japanese army entered and occupied Peking. Soon after, Shanghai fell to the Japanese, followed by Nanjing and Hangkou. As the war escalated, the Nationalist Chiang Kai-shek and the Communist Mao Tse-tung toasted each other and agreed to set aside their personal differences by forming a united front against a common enemy. By this time the conflict had been absorbed into World War II (1939–1945), and Japan's military might was proving insufficient to overcome the problems of guerrilla resistance, insurmountable distances and poor communications in support of their troops.

As Japan's military position deteriorated, the citizens of Manchukuo braced themselves for a Chinese invasion. Nationalist and Communist Chinese armies were poised to move into Manchuria, and the Russians were prowling along the Sino-Russian border. P'u Yi spent sleepless nights pacing back and forth in his room, breaking unlit cigarettes between his fingers. He kept a loaded pistol on him at all times. He knew that if Japan surrendered, Manchuria would be restored to China and that none of the Allies would venture to protect him. But what if the Japanese abandoned him? His anxiety and sleepless nights increased.

On 6 August 1945, the Americans took everyone by surprise when they dropped the atom bomb on Hiroshima. Forty-eight hours later, the Russians invaded Manchuria. When the commander of the Japanese army arrived to report that Soviet troops had crossed the border, P'u Yi went numb with fright. No sooner had he received the news than the air-raid sirens sounded and Russian bombs began exploding near his compound. P'u Yi and his panic-stricken court spent the night cowering in the basement. The following morning a Japanese staff officer arrived to announce the army's plan: the emperor must escape!

Six days later, on the evening of 13 August, P'u Yi and his dwindling entourage boarded a train headed for T'unghua, a mountain retreat near the Korean border. En route, Russian bombs diverted the train to Talitzkou where the imperial party spent the night in an old miners' hostel. As they listened to the radio the following morning, Emperor Hirohito announced Japan's surrender. P'u Yi called a meeting in the hostel dining room. In a solemn ceremony conducted with strict regard for imperial protocol, the Emperor of Manchukuo formally announced his abdication – the third time in his life that he was obliged to renounce his throne. An edict was drawn up and P'u Yi affixed his seal. He then formally acknowledged his ministers and thanked them for their loyalty. In his autobiography he described the event as 'one more farce to be played out'.

The business at hand finished, P'u Yi's former aide announced that they must find their way to T'unghua, where an aeroplane was waiting to fly them to Japan. The plane, he said, was small and limited in seating capacity, so P'u Yi must select eight people only from his entourage. He chose his brother P'u Chieh, two brothers-in-law, three nephews, his personal physician, and his bodyguard Big Li. The empress, Hiro and Jade Lute would sadly have to be left behind. Jade Lute and the empress begged P'u Yi to take them with him. He tried to assure them that arrangements would be made and they would meet again in a few days. In fact, in war-torn Manchukuo at that very moment there were no such arrangements and P'u Yi never saw his empress again.

To P'u Yi's relief, a plane was indeed waiting when they arrived in T'unghua, and it flew them to Mukden, where he thought they were to wait for a connecting aircraft to fly them to Japan.

As they sat in the forlorn airport lounge, the former emperor was immobilized with depression, hunched over in a chair. He did not even react when a squadron of Soviet planes touched down at Mukden airport. Then, before he realized it, his Japanese guards had been disarmed and he was rapidly surrounded by Russian soldiers armed with sub-machine guns. Resigned to his fate, he quietly followed instructions and boarded the plane to which they directed him. As it took off for Siberia, he reflected on Johnston's fateful story of the cold-blooded execution of the Tsar and his entire family and spent the rest of the flight concerned about what the Russians had in store for him.

Back at the mining hostel the women lived in fear, unaware when the enemy would strike. By this time the Communists and the Nationalists had resumed their civil war and at night the women lay awake listening to ever-encroaching gunshots. A month after P'u Yi's departure, the Chinese Communists discovered the abandoned party and placed them under custody. The three women spent the winter in a freezing cell with limited food and water. By April 1946 Jade Lute had been released. Hiro and the empress were not as fortunate. They were sent into detention near the Korean border in a cart

which bore a banner that read 'Traitors from the Manchukuo
Imperial Family'. After two months of being chained together
in a concrete cell, Hiro was released; the empress by then was
too ill to travel. She spent her last days writhing in agony from
the scourge of opium addiction and its withdrawal symptoms
on the floor of her cell. At the end of June 1946, Beautiful
Countenance ascended upon the dragon and joined her
ancestors. She was barely forty years old.

During this period P'u Yi was living in limbo in a health resort
near Khabarovsk. To his surprise, he was being treated civilly as
a guest rather than a prisoner of the Soviet Union. He occupied
private quarters and was assigned attendants to wait on him.
Meals, though frugal, were served three times daily, and
Russian tea was served on the veranda in the afternoon. He had
nurses to care for him; and every morning he was accompanied
on a stroll in the countryside by a Russian armed guard who
addressed him as 'Your Excellency'. It all seemed too good to be
true, but P'u Yi attributed his treatment to either a conspiracy
or an agreement among the Allies. He was unaware that Stalin
was biding his time observing the developments of the Chinese
civil war, secretly hoping that Manchuria would become
independent of China, thus creating an opportunity to

establish a Soviet satellite state. Given the chance, Stalin would use P'u Yi in the same manner the Japanese had done.

In the spring of 1946, P'u Yi was flown to Tokyo to testify as a prosecution witness at the International Military Tribunal for the Far East. For eleven days he sat in the witness box in the wooden-panelled auditorium of the Japanese Military Academy in Tokyo, testifying against the Japanese. The defence counsel was determined to prove that he had willingly collaborated with the Japanese. On the stand, P'u Yi countered by giving an impressive performance, claiming that he had been taken to Manchuria against his will. 'I was not a free man,' he said. The defense lawyer challenged him. What about his old friend Reginald Johnston? Didn't he write in his book *Twilight in the Forbidden City* that 'P'u Yi left Tienstin and went to Manchuria of his own free will'? 'Ridiculous' said P'u Yi. 'Johnston wrote this book with a commercial end in view. I should not be held responsible for what he wrote.' The US prosecutor interceded to contest the use of Johnston's book as evidence since Johnston had passed away in 1938. At this point the president of the tribunal concluded that further cross-examination was 'utterly useless' and ordered P'u Yi to be returned to the Russians in Siberia.

On 1 October 1949 Mao Tse-tung – the leader of the Communist victory over the Nationalists – proclaimed the People's Republic of China and Peking once again became the capital of a new regime. Terrified of being returned to China, P'u Yi sent a plea to the Russian authorities to grant him asylum in Siberia. In return he received no reply. He then begged the general in charge of the health resort in Khabarovsk to allow him to remain in Siberia. But his efforts were in vain – he was no longer of any use to Stalin. Nine months later, the last Manchu emperor of China was handed over to the Chinese Communists. At the border between Siberia and Manchuria, he and his fellow prisoners were welcomed back to 'the Motherland' by a middle-aged man in a drab grey uniform. They had nothing to fear, he told them. They were about to begin a new life in a new China. The small band of prisoners boarded a train headed for the Fushan Detention Centre in Manchuria.

On arrival, they were allotted cells. P'u Yi was relieved to be given a room with P'u Chieh and three of his nephews. But this did not last long. After a few weeks it became clear that at forty-four, P'u Yi was incapable of looking after himself. He had in all his life never been obliged to make his bed, dress himself or tie his shoelaces. Like a faithful servant, P'u Chieh did everything for him. Determined to re-educate and whip him into shape, the wardens separated P'u Yi from his family and placed him in a cell with former officials of Manchukuo. Visibly distressed, P'u Yi returned to his old nervous habit of breaking unlit cigarettes.

For the next nine years, between 1950 and 1959, P'u Yi underwent a rigorous 'thought reform' programme. Many a time he asked himself why the Communists didn't just take his life. The fact was that Mao Tse-tung was aware the last Manchu emperor was more valuable alive than dead to the new China, since Manchuria was not yet under Peking's complete control. But there was more to it than that. As former emperor of the Ch'ing dynasty, P'u Yi represented everything that was evil about the old order. If he could be transformed into an exemplary Communist citizen it would validate the superiority of the new order. So important was P'u Yi's case that Premier Chou En-lai took a personal interest in his re-education.

Although P'u Yi was treated with tacit deference, he was stripped of all privacy and his thoughts became the property of the Communist state. He was indoctrinated with communist ideology and required to write essays in praise of Chairman Mao. As part of his brainwashing, he was asked to write a detailed diary of his life. But this was not an intimate journal. It was read aloud and picked apart during group discussions among fellow political prisoners. Passages of it were written over and over, until the wardens were satisfied that it has been purged of any 'dangerous thoughts'. Eventually, P'u Yi was forced to acknowledge Mao's doctrine in order to preserve his sanity.

It was not purely political conversion that P'u Yi's captors sought – they wanted his soul. They invaded his spiritual sanctuary and tried to destroy his faith in Buddhism. As part of a 'health' campaign against flies, P'u Yi was given a fly swatter. To counter Buddhism's prohibition against killing any living thing, he was ordered to swat as many flies as he could. As a devout Buddhist, P'u Yi believed that the act of taking any life would return to haunt him in his afterlife. Nevertheless he was forced to participate in the fly hunt. Instead of deliberately killing flies, he managed to shoo them out the window. Eventually, the wardens could stand his evasive tactics no longer and forced him to kill a fly. The incident haunted him for weeks after.

In 1956, after seven years of totalitarian rule, China entered a brief period of 'liberalism'. Initiated in the wake of Khruschev's denunciation of Stalin, Chairman Mao launched the Hundred

Flowers Movement to promote public expression in the hope
that mild criticism would shake up inefficient bureaucrats who
were restraining China's progress. In this political climate,
P'u Yi was given more freedom: for the first time in six years,
he was allowed to receive letters and visitors. Through letters
from his relatives, he learned of the empress's death and that
his father had passed away in 1951. When Prince Tsai visited
him, P'u Yi broke down and wept. The family, his uncle told
him, were doing well under the Communists. And Chairman
Mao had told Prince Tsai that he was pleased with P'u Yi's
progress. 'I began 1958 full of hope,' he said. But his hopes were
dashed when fierce attacks on the Communist system itself
prompted Mao to 'weed out' the regime's critics. He spent the
next year being 'reformed' by means of hard labour.

Then, on 14 September 1959, the People's Republic of China
celebrated its tenth anniversary. To mark the occasion
Chairman Mao declared an amnesty for war criminals who had
'truly transformed themselves from an evil past to a virtuous
present.' The next day the prisoners at Fushan attended a
meeting in the auditorium. An official from the Supreme
People's Court mounted the red flag bedecked stage and read
the following notice of special pardon:

The war criminal Aisin Gioro P'u Yi, aged 54,
of Manchu nationality, and from Peking,
has now served ten years' [sic.] detention.
As a result of remoulding through labour
and ideological education he has shown that
he has genuinely reformed. In accordance with
Clause 1 of the Special Pardon Order
he is therefore to be released.

P'u Yi wept.

The Long Journey to Freedom

And so, on 9 December 1959, the Lord of Ten Thousand Years returned to Peking, the city where his tragic life had begun, the city where it would end. At Peking railway station he was met by a crowd of relatives; some he had not seen in years, some he had never met. After an awkward silence, they greeted him as 'elder brother', a form of address they would never have dared use in the days of empire. It was 'the beginning of a new life,' P'u Yi recalled.

Step by step, P'u Yi was guided into a life that would have been utterly unimaginable when he fled Peking thirty-four years earlier. In March 1960, he was assigned as a part-time assistant in Peking's Botanical Gardens. Around the same time, he began working on his autobiography *From Emperor to Citizen*, a project suggested by Chou En-lai and based on his prison diary. The project took four years, during which P'u Yi was transferred to the Chinese People's Political and Consultative Office, where he worked as an archivist researching the Manchu past. He also remarried in 1962, for the fifth time, to Li Shu-shien, a robust Chinese nurse in her forties. The marriage was arranged by Chairman Mao and symbolic in the political sense, for it was the first time in history that a Manchu of the royal blood line had married a Chinese.

Some time after his return to Peking, P'u Yi visited the Forbidden City. He was amazed by its transformation. The secret heart of the Celestial Empire, the world of his childhood, was now a public museum, teeming with visitors. As he entered the imperial gardens, he saw children playing in the winter sun and old men sipping tea in the formal courtyards. He looked up at the golden roof of the Hall of Supreme Harmony where he had been catapulted to the throne in 1908. 'I was sure that the sun was shining brighter here than it had ever done before,' he wrote in his autobiography.

Whether P'u Yi really found happiness in New China, we shall never know. But his past returned to haunt him when the Cultural Revolution erupted in 1966 and once again he was ensnared by the forces of history. During the turmoil (which was rooted in Mao's brutal campaign of ideological cleansing), militant students known as Red Guards stormed the streets brandishing hammers and shouting revolutionary slogans. Armed with copies of Mao's 'Little Red Book', they attacked anything redolent of imperialism, the West and the Soviet Union. Tens of thousands of people were arrested, humiliated, sent to labour camps or executed.

While P'u Yi lay in Peking's Capital Hospital, he learned that the Red Guards had burnt portraits of China's emperors and empresses and smashed Buddhist statues. Ill and distressed, he lay wide awake each night tormented by visions of a slow cruel death. As the wrath of the Red Guards intensified, P'u Yi was denounced in wall posters that appeared all over Peking. Red Guards managed to storm into the hospital and drag P'u Yi out of his ward, but the hospital nurses were under strict orders from Premier Chou En-lai to do all to protect him. To Chou En-lai, the former emperor was an exemplar of Communist remoulding; to the fanatical Red Guards, he was a traitor.

It was only twelve years later, when the madness subsided, and P'u Yi had long passed on, that he was recognized as an honorary citizen of the PRC and his ashes were transferred to the Eight Treasures Cemetery.

History had finally fr